ISBN-10: 1537249304
ISBN-13: 978-1537249308

IGNITE! Quotes to Spark a Love of Learning

Michael Stutman
and Kevin Conklin

DEDICATION

For all the educators in our lives and those who dedicate themselves to creating a inspiring world of learning for young people.

To our wives, Karen and Emily, for their immense commitment to our children's education and learning.

To our teaching mentors, Christine, Joan, Maureen, Andy and Tom for your lifelong commitment to education and 'your' kids.

To the thousands of educators and students who visit InspireMyKids.com each day and keep stoking our fires with feedback and enthusiasm.

For the greater thinkers and people represented in this book, for their incredible wisdom and foresight.

For our children (Ryan, Anna, Danny, Sean, Jason, Andrew and Lily) whose unique passions, learning styles and curiosities put the importance of education in front of us every day.

For our parents—Bill, Nancy, Walter, and Joan—who taught us the importance of having a love of learning.

We thank you all from the bottoms of our hearts.

Mike and Kevin

INTRODUCTION

A Note to Children

Becoming the best version of yourself and helping to change the world involves becoming a lifelong learner.

And quotes can be an incredible fuel for your daily fire. They can shine a light on new ways of thinking, reveal how successful people handled their own learning, and inspire you in a fast and fun way.

Many quotes on the pages that follow come from people who have made a big difference in the world. As you will see, one common thing that binds them together is not just their impact, but their love of learning.

This book focuses on connecting a love of learning to passion and good habits. Our hope is that it will, in some small way, help you on your journey to become a lifelong learner and a difference maker in the world.

The good news, for today, is that even small actions and small changes to the way you think and learn can have a huge impact on your life and the world. So don't wait! Start today—get inspired, keep learning and practice taking positive actions every day.

And who knows, maybe someday your name will appear after a quote or two on these pages!

We wish you all the best.

INTRODUCTION

A Note to Adults & Educators

The inspiring words and people found in this book are at the heart of what we do at InspireMyKids.

Our unwavering goal is to share inspiring, age-appropriate, real-life stories, quotes, media, and projects that help children become the best they can be and take positive action to make the world a better place.

We have focused this collection of quotes on topics to help inspire learning. We selected quotes based on their potential appeal to children and then validated based on feedback by children.

Whether you are an educator, parent, coach or mentor, we trust you will find inspiration in these pages. Thank you for your desire to help kids learn and make the world a better place.

We also hope that you will join us on the InspireMyKids (IMK) journey at our home–the world's largest community of inspiration for kids–http://inspiremykids.com.

And if you like this book, please check out The Ultimate Book of Inspiring Quotes for Kids on Amazon.com!

Mike Stutman and the IMK Team

Co-founder and Dad

www.inspiremykids.com
mike@inspiremykids.com

TABLE OF CONTENTS

The 100+ quotes in this book are organized into 3 sessions:

InspireMyKids.com

EDUCATION & LEARNING

Education and learning are two of the most important ingredients to becoming all that you can be. How open you are to learning will help determine your path in life.

Education does not just happen at school. It is not just about math and other subjects. Learning is happening all the time, whenever your mind is open.

Education is not just about learning facts but more so about learning how to think. It is learning to make good choices. It is learning to act with purpose.

Becoming educated is a lifelong process. It can be hard and frustrating at times, but it can also be incredibly exciting and enriching. Most importantly, learning and education can help you to achieve the following:

- Change the world
- Become your best self
- Reach your potential
- Eliminate your fears
- Make the most of your mistakes
- Support your family

Here are some inspiring quotes that capture the power of education and its potential to impact you and the world:

"Education is the most powerful weapon which you can use to change the world"

– Nelson Mandela

"When you know better you do better"

– Maya Angelou

"Somewhere, something incredible is waiting to be known"

– Carl Sagan

"Even the wisest mind has something yet to learn"

– George Santayana

"Anyone who stops learning is old, whether at twenty or eighty. Anyone who keeps learning stays young"

– Henry Ford

"The important thing is not to stop questioning"

– Albert Einstein

"Learning is a treasure that will follow its owner everywhere"

– Chinese proverb

"None of us is as smart as all of us"

– Ken Blanchard

"A house is not a home unless it contains food and fire for the mind as well as the body"

– Benjamin Franklin

"The mind is not a vessel to be filled, but a fire to be kindled"

– Plutarch

"Educating the mind without educating the heart is no education at all"

– Aristotle

"You can tell whether a man is clever by his answers. You can tell whether a man is wise by his questions"

– Naguib Mahfouz

"Education is not the filling of a pail, but the lighting of a fire"

– W. B. Yeats

"If you can't explain it simply, you don't understand it well enough"

– Albert Einstein

"Nothing in life is to be feared. It is only to be understood"

– Marie Curie

"A mistake is a crash-course in learning"

– Billy Anderson

"We are not what we know but what we are willing to learn"

– Mary Catherine Bateson

"He who opens a school door, closes a prison"

– Victor Hugo

"Knowledge will bring you the opportunity to make a difference"

– Claire Fagan

"Education is teaching our children to desire the right things"

– Plato

"I believe that we learn by practice. Whether it means to learn to dance by practicing dancing or to learn to live by practicing living, the principles are the same. Practice means to perform, over and over again in the face of all obstacles, some act of vision, of faith, of desire. Practice is a means of inviting the perfection desired"

— Martha Graham

"Education is the power to think clearly, the power to act well in the world's work, and the power to appreciate life"

— Brigham Young

"I received the fundamentals of my education in school, but that was not enough. My real education, the superstructure, the details, the true architecture, I got out of the public library. For an impoverished child whose family could not afford to buy books, the library was the open door to wonder and achievement, and I can never be sufficiently grateful that I had the wit to charge through that door and make the most of it"

— Isaac Asimov

"Painful as it may be, a significant emotional event can be the catalyst for choosing a direction that serves us—and those around us—more effectively. Look for the learning"

— Louisa May Alcott

"Imagination is more important than knowledge. For knowledge is limited to all we now know and understand, while imagination embraces the entire world, and all there ever will be to know and understand"

– Albert Einstein

READING

Reading is fundamental. In fact, it is one of the most important ingredients to becoming all that you can be.

Reading develops your brain, provides a window into the world around you, and helps you do better in all school subjects.

Most importantly, reading can help you become not only a better student but also a better person. You can learn from the brightest people whenever and wherever you choose.

As important as reading is, did you know that eight hundred million people around the world cannot read or write, and many families (and some schools) have no books for children to read?

There are likely many children and people in your town or city that fall into this group. Maybe someday you will be in a position to help them.

In the meantime, here are some inspiring quotes that bring to life the power of reading and reveal its ability to make you a better person:

"Once you learn to read, you will be forever free"

— Frederick Douglass

"The more that you read, the more things you will know. The more you learn, the more places you'll go"

— Dr. Seuss

"I find television very educating. Every time somebody turns on the set, I go into the other room and read a book"

— Groucho Marx

"There are many little ways to enlarge your world. Love of books is the best of all"

— Jacqueline Kennedy

"Today a reader, tomorrow a leader"

— Margaret Fuller

"There is more treasure in books than in all the pirates loot on Treasure Island"

— Walt Disney

"There are worse crimes than burning books. One of them is not reading them"

— Ray Bradbury

"Reading without reflecting is like eating without digesting"

— Edmund Burke

"The reading of all good books is like conversation with the finest people of the past centuries"

— Descartes

"Reading is to the mind what exercise is to the body"

— Richard Steele

"So please, oh PLEASE, we beg, we pray, go throw your TV set away, And in its place you can install, a lovely bookshelf on the wall"

— Roald Dahl

"Reading is a discount ticket to everywhere"

— Mary Schmich

"Books are a uniquely portable magic"

— Stephen King

"No entertainment is so cheap as reading, nor any pleasure so lasting"

— Lady Mary Wortley Montagu

"To learn to read is to light a fire"

— Victor Hugo

WRITING & STORYTELLING

"After nourishment, shelter and companionship, stories are the things we need most in the world."

–Phillip Pullman

You may not yet believe it, but writing and storytelling have the power to change your life and the lives of others. Your writing skills will impact what college you go to, what career you pursue, and how much of an impact you have on the world.

Writing and storytelling are not easy. They take effort, time, practice, and the courage to begin. They provide a way to express what you love and what excites you. They are a way to escape and create the world the way you would like it be.

The sooner you understand the power of writing and storytelling, and the power of building these skills, the better off you will be.

Check out these inspiring quotes about writing and then take action with our resources below:

"No tears in the writer, no tears in the reader. No surprise in the writer, no surprise in the reader"

— Robert Frost

"Be yourself. Above all, let who you are, what you are, what you believe, shine through every sentence you write, every piece you finish"

— John Jakes

"All that I hope to say in books, all that I ever hope to say, is that I love the world"

— E. B. White

"If there's a book that you want to read, but it hasn't been written yet, then you must write it"

— Toni Morrison

"I can shake off everything as I write; my sorrows disappear, my courage is reborn"

— Anne Frank

"You don't write because you want to say something, you write because you have something to say"

— F. Scott Fitzgerald

"So the writer who breeds more words than he needs, is

making a chore for the reader who reads"

— Dr. Seuss

"I kept always two books in my pocket, one to read, one to write in"

— Robert Louis Stevenson

"My aim is to put down on paper what I see and what I feel in the best and simplest way"

— Ernest Hemingway

"The most valuable of all talents is that of never using two words when one will do"

— Thomas Jefferson

"Fill your paper with the breathings of your heart"

— William Wadsworth

"Almost all good writing begins with terrible first efforts. You need to start somewhere"

— Anne Lamott

"All I need is a sheet of paper and something to write with, and then I can turn the world upside down"

— Friedrich Nietzsche

"Easy reading is hard writing"

— Nathaniel Hawthorne

"I love writing. I love the swirl and swing of words as they tangle with human emotions"

— James A. Michener

"Write the kind of story you would like to read. People will give you all sorts of advice about writing, but if you are not writing something you like, no one else will like it either"

— Meg Cabot

"The true alchemists do not change lead into gold; they change the world into words"

— William H. Gass

"Start writing, no matter what. The water does not flow until the faucet is turned on"

— Louis L'Amour

"The scariest moment is always just before you start"

— Stephen King

"If you want to be a writer, you must do two things

above all others: read a lot and write a lot"

— Stephen King

"You can make anything by writing"

— C. S. Lewis

"I write to give myself strength. I write to be the characters that I am not. I write to explore all the things I'm afraid of"

— Joss Whedon

"You can't wait for inspiration. You have to go after it with a club"

— Jack London

"The most difficult thing about writing; is writing the first line"

— Amit Kalantri

"There is nothing to writing. All you do is sit down at a typewriter and bleed"

— Ernest Hemingway

PASSION & ENTHUSIASM

What are the things in school and in life that get you most excited? Maybe you like sports, animals, music, Legos, writing, cars, or helping people. Do you have something that you are passionate about? If so, you are very lucky! If not, don't worry—you just need to pay attention to what you like and dislike and be open to trying new things. Having passion and enthusiasm is key for achieving success and meaning in school and life. As Arthur Balfour once said, "Enthusiasm moves the world."

Here are other great quotes about the importance and roles of passion and enthusiasm in life:

"Find something you're passionate about and keep tremendously interested in it"

— Julia Child

"I have no special talents. I am only passionately curious"

— Albert Einstein

"Every great dream begins with a dreamer. Always remember, you have within you the strength, the patience, and the passion to reach for the stars to change the world"

— Harriet Tubman

"Feel your emotions, Live true your passions, Keep still your mind"

— Geoffrey Gluckman

"Passion is a feeling that tells you: this is the right thing to do. Nothing can stand in my way. It doesn't matter what anyone else says. This feeling is so good that it cannot be ignored"

— Wayne Dyer

"There is no passion to be found playing small—in settling for a life that is less than the one you are capable of living"

— Nelson Mandela

"Develop a passion for learning. If you do, you will never cease to grow"

— Anthony D'Angelo

"Passion is what drives us crazy, what makes us do extraordinary things, to discover, to challenge ourselves. Passion is and should always be the heart of courage"

— Midori Komatsu

"Be brave and be patient. Have faith in yourself; trust in the significance of your life and the purpose of your passion"

— Jillian Michaels

"Passion is energy. Feel the power that comes from focusing on what excites you"

— Oprah Winfrey

"Enthusiasm is one of the most powerful engines of success. When you do a thing, do it with all your might. Put your whole soul into it. Stamp it with your own personality. Be active, be energetic and faithful, and you will accomplish your object. Nothing great was ever achieved without enthusiasm"

— Ralph Waldo Emerson

"No matter what you do with your life, be passionate"

— Jon Bon Jovi

"Rest in reason; move in passion"

— Khalil Gibran

"Don't ask yourself what the world needs; ask yourself what makes you come alive. And then go and do that. Because what the world needs is people who have come alive"

— Howard Thurman

"A person can succeed at almost anything for which they have unlimited enthusiasm"

— Charles Schwab

"'Why do we have to listen to our hearts?' the boy asked, when they had made camp that day. 'Because, wherever your heart is, that is where you'll find your treasure'"

— Paulo Cohelmo

"Doing what you love isn't a privilege; it's an obligation"

— Barbara Sher

InspireMyKids.com

HARD WORK & DOING YOUR BEST

Sometimes doing your best work or trying your hardest at something is difficult. It may have to do with trying to do something new for the first time, like a new sport or activity at school. It may have to do with doing homework for a subject that is not your favorite or is not your best.

As Hunter S. Thompson once said, "Anything worth doing, is worth doing right." And as Albert Einstein added, "We have to do the best we can. This is our sacred human responsibility."

Developing the habits of trying your hardest and doing your best work is something that will help you succeed throughout your life. Have you have ever tried to take a shortcut and do something fast, but not well? Most of the time, the result is that you need to do it over again. And then it takes twice as long!

So, take a moment to learn from the wisdom of the quotes below. There is no doubt that following this advice will serve you well in life over and over again!

"Little by little one walks far"

— Peruvian proverb

"You should always be well and bright, for so you do your best work; and you have so much beautiful work to do. The world needs it, and you must give it!"

— Marie Correlli

"We have to do the best we can. This is our sacred human responsibility"

— Albert Einstein

"I do the very best I know, the very best I can, and I mean to keep on doing so until the end"

— Abraham Lincoln

"Do your best when no one is looking. If you do that, then you can be successful at anything you put your mind to"

— Bob Cousy

"A problem is a chance for you to do your best"

— Duke Ellington

"If you try to do your best, there is no failure"

— Mike Farrell

"Whatever you are, be a good one"

— Abraham Lincoln

"Doing your best means never stop trying"

— Benjamin Franklin

"Just Do It"

— Nike

"The best preparation for tomorrow is doing your best today"

— H. Jackson Brown

"Don't be afraid to give your best to what seemingly are small jobs. Every time you conquer one it makes you that much stronger. If you do little jobs well, the big ones will tend to take care of themselves"

— Dale Carnegie

"If you do things well, do them better. Be daring, be first, be different, be just"

— Anita Roddick

"Doing your best at this moment puts you in the best place for the next moment"

— Oprah Winfrey

"You must do the thing you think you cannot do"

— Eleanor Roosevelt

"Make the most of yourself, for that is all there is of you"

— Ralph Waldo Emerson

"Do right. Do your best. Treat others the way you want to be treated"

— Lou Holtz

"No effort that we take to attain something beautiful is ever lost"

— Helen Keller

"People pretend not to like grapes when the vines are too high for them to reach"

— Margueritte de Navarre

"So early in my life, I had learned that if you want something, you had better make some noise"

— Malcolm X

"If you're not going to go all the way, why go at all?"

— Joe Namath

"Do the best you can in every task, no matter how unimportant it may seem at the time"

— Sandra Day O'Connor

"Advancement only comes with habitually doing more than you are asked"

— Gary Ryan Blair

"When you reach the top, keep climbing"

— proverb

"When we do the best that we can, we never know what miracle is wrought in our life, or in the life of another"

— Helen Keller

"Do more than is required. What is the distance between someone who achieves their goals consistently and those who spend their lives and careers merely following? The extra mile"

— Gary Ryan Blair

SUCCESS

What is success and how do you define success in your life? Everyone seems to think about it quite differently!

While some people think that money or happiness equals success, other people measure it by how much help they provide to others. Here are even more ways to think about success:

- Living a life you can be proud of
- Giving your all
- Standing up for things that are right even when it's hard
- Becoming the best version of yourself

As Albert Einstein even suggest that you should not be a person of success this famous quote of his: "Try not to become a man of success. Rather become a man of value."

Now read some of the inspiring success quotes below and think about what success means to you.

"Success is not the key to happiness. Happiness is the key to success. If you love what you are doing, you will be successful."

– Herman Cain

"The level of our success is limited only by our imagination and no act of kindness, however small, is ever wasted."

– Aesop

"Success is peace of mind, which is a direct result of self-satisfaction in knowing you did your best to become the best you are capable of becoming."
– John Wooden

"Success means having the courage, the determination, and the will to become the person you believe you were meant to be."

– George Sheehan

"Success comes in cans; failure in can'ts."

– Wilfred Peterson

"There are no secrets to success. It is the result of preparation, hard work, and learning from failure."

– Colin Powell

Success is a ladder that cannot be climbed with your hands in your pocket."

— Mark Caine

"The dictionary is the only place where success comes before work."

— Mark Twain

"There is no elevator to success. You have to take the stairs."

— Anonymous

"The price of success is hard work, dedication to the job at hand, and the determination that whether we win or lose, we have applied the best of ourselves to the task at hand."

— Vince Lombardi

"Success doesn't come to you - you go to it!"

— Marva Collins

"There's no limit to what a person can achieve if they don't care who gets the credit."

— J. Laing Burns, Jr.

"Seventy percent of success in life is showing up."

— Woody Allen

CONCLUSION

We hope you found this book to be inspiring and that many of the quotes in this book spoke to you. Perhaps one of the ideas will help you or a child in your life to take positive action toward change.

We also hope that this is the beginning, not the end, of our interaction with you. If you like what you found in this book, please consider joining InspireMyKids on our journey to help children become their best and make the world a better place.

To stay abreast of new quotes that we compile, books we publish, and real-life, inspiring stories and projects for kids, please visit our website—www.inspiremykids.com—to sign up for our e-mail list and connect with us on social media.

Also, the educator section of our website includes ideas to start incorporating inspirational quotes into your school or class and access to worksheets and common core lesson plans.

Lastly, we truly welcome your feedback:

- What book would you like to see us publish next?
- How could we make this book more valuable?
- What quote topics do you want us to explore next?
- Do you have a favorite quote you would like us to include in our next edition or book?

Please send your thoughts, feedback, and ideas to info@inspiremykids.com.

Thanks again for joining us on this journey.

Mike Stutman and the IMK Team

Co-founder and Dad

www.inspiremykids.com

mike@inspiremykids.com